PRAISE FOR OUR WILD MAGIC

"Amanda Linsmeier writes with the sort of naked candor that is just as sobering as it is whimsical. Reading *Our Wild Magic* was like sitting down to tea with an old friend—one who has just returned from holiday in the Underworld." —Morgan Nickola-Wren, author of *Magic With Skin On*

"Linsmeier's writing is eloquent and raw, with a sprinkle of enchantment. Her talent for crafting poetry shines through in this alluring collection." —Shelby Leigh, author of *It Starts Like This*

"Quietly powerful, *Our Wild Magic* delves into the heart of womanhood with a tender sincerity that kept me turning the pages. Among my favorite poems in the collection were those that defied expectation by turning well-known fairytale tropes on their head. *Our Wild Magic* is a wonderful balancing act between shorter, bite-sized poems and longer works that demand the reader's complete attention in order to truly savor the nuances of Amanda Linsmeier's writing." —N.L. Shompole, author of *Lace, Bone, Beast: Poems & Other Fairytale for Wicked Girls*

"In the same way fairytales speak to us with their wildness, cruelty, and bright hope, Linsmeier's poems use beautiful imagery of magic and myth to illustrate our everyday human emotions. They soothed and inspired me, for while anxiety and fear are the deep dark forest, the right words are the spell that can fix us, whether we're the wronged hero or the wicked witch—and of course all of us contain both." —Molly Ringle, author of *The Goblins of Bellwater*

"*Our Wild Magic* is a stunning follow-up to Amanda Linsmeier's debut poetry collection, *Like Waves*. Amanda uses the pen as a light to expose the unvarnished truth about all facets of not just the human experience, but *her* human experience. The same hand that writes about the tragedy of miscarriage is the same hand that writes about the laurels of motherhood and self-love. Amanda does not leave you without water, even as she walks you through the most arid times in her life—and to me, that is the wildest magic of all."
—Marya Layth, author of *More Than Bread*

"Linsmeier has once again shown her ability to be authentic and honest through *Our Wild Magic*."
—The Literary Birds

"*Our Wild Magic* enchanted me with a magic of its own. Some poems lured me into a mystical world created by the author, while others reached inside me, calling like to like." —Jamie McLachlan, author of *Night Song*

"*Our Wild Magic* is truly a magical read. Her words pour off the page and dive deep into the soul of the reader. Every emotion you can imagine is found woven throughout her pages. The only way to describe *Our Wild Magic* is, simply, phenomenal." —Autumn Lindsey, author of *Remaining Aileen*.

our wild magic

POEMS

Amanda Linsmeier

Our Wild Magic
Amanda Linsmeier

Published by Emerald Lily Publishing
Copyright © 2018, 2020 Amanda Linsmeier
Cover Art by Ampersand Book Covers

I Ask For Love previously published by Moonchild Magazine
Wild Magic & *Curses* previously published by Fireflies & Fairy
Dust: A Fantasy Anthology
Goddess previously published in Poetic Pairings pamphlet
Artwork and photography by Amanda Linsmeier

2nd Edition
ISBN 13 978-0-9987705-5-0

DEDICATION

to the wild ones, no matter how much you've been tamed

&

to the three little beasties who help me to see magic every day

TABLE OF CONTENTS

A NOTE FOR YOU

Within each section of this book, you'll find decidedly different themes, from the twisted to the playful, and the sections are told, more or less, in a chronological portrayal of my mid-teens until my mid-thirties, although I've taken the liberty of adjusting certain poems to fit within more appropriate themes. If I felt possible, I left the timeline intact. Although there are poems inspired by others (including a few black-out poems), most of the things within this collection are my own emotions and experiences, and within these pages I explore love in many forms, mental health including anxiety and depression, beauty and self-esteem, sexuality, nature, adulthood, healing.

As a word of caution, some subjects may be sensitive for some readers. Still, though it's deeply personal to me, I hope you'll find yourself welcome in my words.

cursed

my heart crushed under a lover's boots * a visit to the
emergency room because I can't breathe * the death of dreams
* going to sleep so I don't have to feel * the taste of charcoal *
my heaving chest * being lonely in a crowd * losing myself *
losing everything * giving everything away * my tear-soaked
pillow * uncontrollable thoughts * a hollow feeling in my gut *
the smell of hospital antiseptic * sickly sweet perfume *
desperation in my veins * hating my mirror * stale cigarette
smoke * sad songs on repeat * fake smiles * waking up crying
from a good dream * lying when someone asks how I am *
agreeing when someone nicknames me ms. misery * forgetting
my voice * living for someone else and not myself * not fitting
in my own skin * when everyone is a stranger * when I wonder
if I'm even alive * the stench of dying roses * shaking on a
brown couch * my spark going out like a damp match * dark
circles under my eyes * closing the curtains against the sunlight
* a black hole in my chest * being numb with fear * weeping
on the bathroom floor at two a.m. * salt on my tongue * old
letters I can't throw away * a white sky *

POMEGRANATES

the underworld is not a place.
it is a feeling, a sensation, like a prison,
though instead of bars, the teeth
bared beneath his smile
hold me captive.
he is not a reality, but a shadow,
one who took from me
—who *stole*—who reached through me,
to take *me*,
to take what I would never willingly give,
except I did, except I handed him the key
and let him swallow it.

and all above this world blossoms rain
down, and the sweet smell of pomegranates hangs
on the air, taunting me
with a freedom I doubt I'll ever grasp again.
his eyes, his voice, the sharp sketch
of his outline looming
against every dawn...

                    the hours are endless
        when you can't escape the prison
                    you've made yourself,
        when you can't escape the prison
                    you've let someone else
                        make for you.

3

SIREN SONG
black-out poem, adapted from Douglas Dunn's Landlocked

I am waiting for
the sea.
I can't remember listening
for dead longings
before.

waiting, I listen
to the winding, small noises,
ships at night, sailing out
to where the sea
is missing.

FEATHER

today a feather blew across
my path,
soft gray kissing
the summer grass, and I thought,
what kind of bird left that?
was it shed willingly or taken?
or was it merely a symbol of the way we rip ourselves
apart for love?

(like Odette, with the spell laid upon her,
grief-stricken, molting with longing)

imagine changing from something whole
to something strewn across the ground—

have you?

imagine leaving bits of yourself behind,
losing yourself piece by piece.

MIRAGE

here was the mirage:

his eyes full of salt,
his mouth water-wet,
rain and love pouring
from him, falling onto the
scorched sand beneath his
flawless feet.

here was the reality:

me there, dry-throated
and thirsty, mouth empty,
desperate for the words
on his weeping tongue.

the sad truth:

not once did he press
his lips to mine.
not once did he ease
the burn in my throat
or in my heart.

the sadder truth:

not once did I ask him to.

PRINCE OF THIEVES

my nights have lost
their meaning
since he left,
since he tore my heart
from the chest

that I foolishly
kept unlocked.

TRICKS & TRADES

for you I threw seeds into a fire's flame,
for you I slept with a slice of wedding cake
under my pillow,
for you I peeled an apple to see
what letter it made,
for you I bathed in milk
and petals,
I oiled, painted,
powdered, curled, shaved,
dyed myself—*died* myself, I killed
all the parts of me
I was afraid were just enough ugly
to push you away.
for you I explored little tricks, hid little flaws,
for you
I made magic,
not in fruit or flame,
or buttercream-scented dreams
but in the way I changed who I was
for you, I made the trade—

me for someone better.

8

MEDICATED

this gnawing hunger in me
is silenced,
though the thirst increases tenfold,
and now I drink so much water
I believe I must be
part mermaid.

think of the little mermaid,
and how she spliced
herself in half
for a pair of shapely legs.
what would I slice
off myself
for beauty, for affection,
for self-love?

this rumbling in me is silenced, I silence
it myself,
and it leaves
the sound of
my over-beating heart
drumming
through my too-human
chest.

ROYAL SEAMSTRESS

I laced myself

into his hands

then was all surprised

when he

u n t h r e a d e d

me.

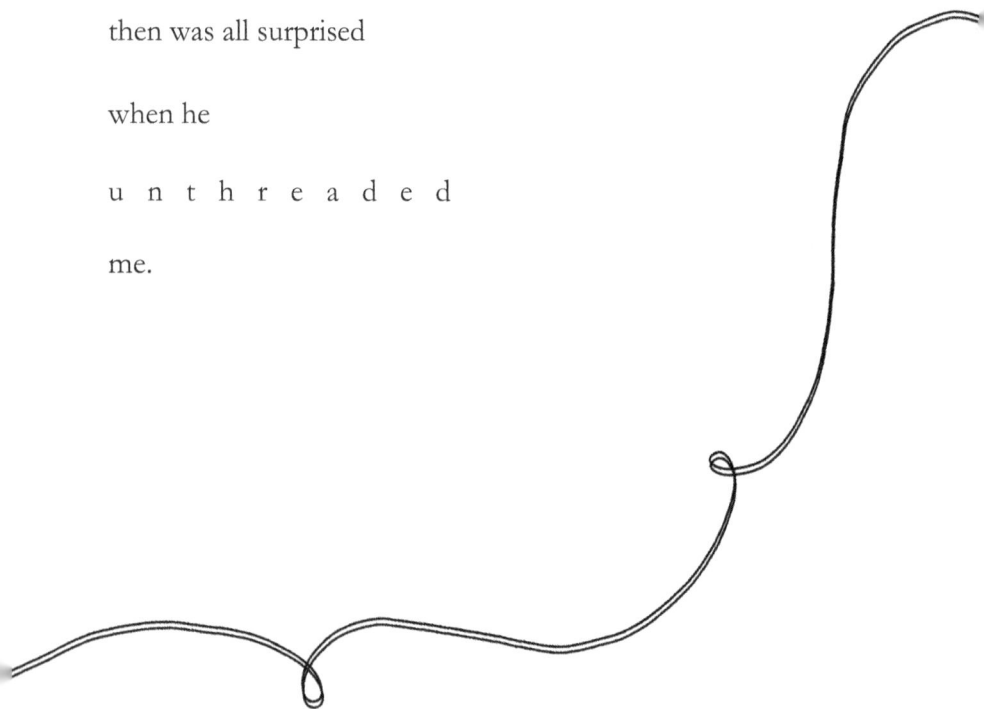

CLOAKED

cloak me,
tuck me under your mantle
of night, crimson staining
my lips, poison snaking
your tongue, wrap me
with your whispered lies,
bind your fingers 'round my life,
hide me,
hide me from this world.

I'll take all the hurt you have to give
over dangers I don't know.

INVISIBILITY

I think the worst curse,
she said,
is to love someone
who doesn't even see you.

SHIPWRECKED

sometimes I think / I carry whole oceans
inside myself
/ the crash of water against
my very soul / my bones rattling with the shock
of storms / dreams buried
like shipwrecks / this casing of me closing
too tight
around the turbulence
within /
this constant tug inside /

the way the sea breathes
after a violent rush
of waves /
how can one body
hold so much
trauma / and not contain whole worlds
inside?

DESPERATION

call it unrequited, call it desperation. this is the despair that
makes up our name. don't our bones echo with it now?

lonely girls, we taste of shame.

here,
take me, take our joy, take every morsel
we can give up, we will starve ourselves for you,
make myself a joke, a pauper, a prayer,
pin our own wings
against the board, cut our bodies up into
stars, sew our lips shut,
exchange our voices for yours.
can't you speak for us, can't you breathe
for us?
our hearts already beat for you.

MAD BOTANTIST

if I close my eyes: his scent haunts my hours,
the hunger of him, skin slick with powers,
the dig of fingers in my roots, my flowers,
he took me apart petal by petal
this memory sours...

I don't want to remember how
I let myself be destroyed, how I let
myself be uprooted,
how I turned my
cheek and gave it all
a pretty name.
amare.

LOST SOULS
black-out poem, adapted from Burial at Sea by Stephen Mulrine

we weep, for us and no one.

we sink,

softness gone,

we grow smaller,

skies dulled, dark ocean,

heart behind us, into eternity,

empty, dead.

A SPELL TO BANISH NEGATIVITY

there isn't one.

wicked

refusing to feel * anger * my one-track mind * planning
revenge I'll never enact * dark clothes * bright flames *
nightmares I cause myself * nightmares I'd like to cause
someone else * self-hate * rage that burns * being so afraid I
turn cold * self-preservation at all costs * laughing at love *
scoffing at happiness * black boots with thick heels * sharp
nails * smoking too much * drinking too much * not giving a
fuck * closing off my heart * sneers * an echo in the night *
accepting my state of being * tricking myself into believing it's
power * selfishness * a cackle * bone-white * swirling shadows
* when I'm green with jealousy * when I can't stop * when I
don't even want to * the wicked witch * betrayal * blades *
cloaks * midnight * a starless sky * ink-black smoke * sharp
teeth * the smell of decay * thorns * falling from grace *
driving past that house at night * screaming into the wind *
nothingness *

QUEEN OF HEARTS

a knife through the heart,
a hole in my chest,
only the worst
can come from the best.
my want has a color,
it is bitter and red.
I keep running your words
past the pain in my head.
a knife through the heart,
a hole in my chest,
roses are crimson,
and love is a test.

JEALOUSY

give me your gilded words,
your tatted ivory lace,
I'll take your pinkened blush,
and snatch your pretty face.

give me your honey voice,
then hide inside your cage.
I'll take your joyful joys
and trade you all my rage.

give me the bright you have,
I want all you can share.
I'll take arms of flowers
then steal your curled hair.

teach me your lovely smile
then show me how you frown.
I'll pull the strong you have
then seize your golden crown.

CURSES
an ode to the Wicked Witch of the West

don't let them tell you that your words mean
nothing,
that you are an empty-mouth,
a pair of green
shaking hands with nothing left to offer.
don't let them tell you that
because you weren't born with silver slippers,
with a road to travel along when you want to
run from one life to another,
that you are not worthy.
you don't need an emerald city, a band of misfit
friends to wander with you on your wanderlust
adventure.
you are made of lonely stuff,
and lonely can be powerful if it lasts long enough,
and power can turn even fragile words
into something that can twist whole houses astray.
you can forge your own roads that way.

a brain, a heart, courage, a home?
you have that all in spades, my dear.
if they cannot see it then curses to them.

FRANKENSTEIN

she's lived through nightmares
(survived, more like).
piece by piece, learned to breath,
held by a body that betrayed her,
let the blood stream
through her fingers, felt herself round
and deflate,
her hopes get all concave,
all her tender faith get scraped away,
her voice grown cold, choked out
with shock and sorrys that weren't hers
to give.
she's lived, with a heart busted and taped
back together, felt like her organs were
borrowed from a stranger, lived with hurt,
with rage, sewed herself shut with silence
because no words could be a weapon, too.

she's lived through a body that was made as though
from nothing but leftover bits of brokenness,
a hand-me-down
form, a second-rate creation.
is it any wonder for so long she felt
like a monster?

MY VILLAIN

my villain was a hot pink mini skirt
—cotton sateen— and a pair of strappy, platform
sandals which I wore all that summer.
my villain was the odor of hair-remover, pink candies,
cheap beer and stale Marlboro Lights,
which I bought for just over
$3 a pack from that little corner gas station
on Geele Avenue.
my villain was a cream-city-brick apartment,
the backseat of his car, the front seat of his car,
my scale, my pathetic longing, the lies I told myself,
the truths I wouldn't tell myself.
my villain was the pool table at that bar
tucked out in the country, and which burned down
years later, as if to cover my regret with ashes.
my villain was his best friend,
a study night turned into something
I could use to make him sorry.
my villain was my brain,
my thoughts, the need crawling up and
down and up and down my naked skin,
the loop of his words in my ear, stuck in my hair,
digging in my bone. my villain was those very bones,
all the organs they protected, when I couldn't
or wouldn't, even protect myself, my
villain was my lips, my mouth,
my hands, all moving toward
the things that would undo everything I could be.

my villain, mostly, was me.

MIRROR, MIRROR

if she dares to look at you
I'll make her sorry she's alive.

nothing will keep that girl safe
from the pain that I'll contrive.

yes, you believe I'm good,
bet it comes as a surprise,

sometimes I'd like to scratch out
both her pretty eyes.

I bet you think I'm sweet,
not a violent bone within,

you'd never guess I shake and seethe
beneath this silky skin.

ETERNAL

did you think this was a fairytale? did you think you'd
be breathless and trembling for the soft tangle
of fingers through your oft-conditioned locks? did you think
you would be bold and fearless, arrows strung across
your satin-back as you slung yourself out into the world?

no. this is bigger, wider-reaching, the way you can't unsee how
you've turned from the pure to the wicked.

this is the reality of the page that keeps flipping when you turn
into your own antagonist. this is not a story anymore now;
it is life, and it lasts forever.

RAPUNZEL

have you seen the way he watches her?

that tilt of a smile on his full lips,
the soft of his eyes flashing
at her legs, her hips,
her hair—long, blond, shining
like a coin.

sometimes, in secret,
I think about finding her in the night
and taking shears to that mane.

I wouldn't do this for rampions
not for riches, nor honor,

I'd ruin her, ruin myself
to cut away at anything that grows
between my goals and me.

THE CAPTAIN
(or, I STILL LOVE KILLIAN JONES)

he went to a place to forget,
but still he carried with him a crescent
like the moon, still heard that sound
whistling
in the night, ticking
through his chest,
stuttering across the sky
like an echo.

the noises, the noises leave him
lonely;
there's nothing left but his
conscience,
and it is not a friendly face.

even he can ache, you know.
feelings don't die just because
you kill them.

promise of a new moon * wildflowers * any flowers * me questioning the catechism teacher * reading witch books in secret * liking the prostitutes' corsets and thigh-highs * the swell of cleavage * the flash of a grin * a chin raised in the air * mother nature * briar rose * bucking tradition * embracing the misfits * stars * sunset * a feral feeling * not fitting in * not wanting to * unbidden laughter * that fine line between being good and bad * the crack of thunder * wild horses * the hum of a tattoo gun * learning to love all the things that are wrong * learning to recognize all the things that are right * my teeth clicking hungrily * a smirk * a flirtatious wink * knowing my power * sharing it *

THUNDERSTORMS

we lived in a big house,
wide spread of field off to the left
where we parked our cars,
even though it wasn't ours,
and I would go run in that field as rain
rained down on me,
as it drenched my hair, my clothes,
wishing I was naked, white flowers strung
in the cloud of my dark hair,
laughing, wet arms outstretched, to welcome
the wild, to invite it in,
to celebrate, to say,

yes, I am here, too

and someday I will rain down like this,

a free, beautiful, truth, knowing

how to make a mess

how to grow things, too,

how to be the kind of expression that

heals, how to be the kind of force

that puts people on their knees,

that makes them

want to beg for more.

HER SECRET

they don't see her wild,
she will stay hidden forever.

under her pure-white gown
she wears scarlet petticoats.

and I'm the only one who glances down
to see them rustle near her dainty feet.

I'm the only one who sees the way
her lashes rest on the curve
of her powdered cheek,
not because she's coy,
but because she has to tame
what hides inside her.

I'm the only one who hears
her cry, *let me out let me out*

even when her rosebud
lips are clamped shut.

I ONCE MET A PRINCE

at the edge of a forest,
I once met a prince on a white horse
and he sailed in and said,
in a posh voice (but not-so-princely fashion):

hey baby, come on over tonight.

what he wanted was for me
to kick up my skirts and part my legs,
to climb astride his
horse,
and go to his castle.
he wanted me to let him
inside.
instead, I smiled sweetly
turned back to the woods, plucked
a piece of heavy
fruit from a tree, took a bite,
let the juice drip
down my creamy
throat
as he watched me hungrily,

as I took something I wanted,

as I didn't let him have me.

TO BE WILD

to be wild first meant to be strong,
and to be that meant
closing off my heart, locking
it up in a cage where no one else
could ~~hurt it~~ brutalize it.
and then I let the vines grown round
my bars, yes, thorns and briars, but
wildflowers too, and slowly
I left the cage door open, so I could
come and go as I pleased.
to be wild meant then that
belief returned again, that
I celebrated my freedom, that I flew
when I wanted,
and if I felt like clipping
my own wings, well, damn it,
I would.

LOVE LETTER
TO THE EARTH

shake me out of this gray living,
shake me out of my own shoes,
the way I've been standing
here, static in one spot.

shake me out of this
resignation,
the six a.m. wake-up calls, the
narrow worry lines etched into my face.

shake me from this boredom
because fear is nothing if not predictable.

shake me like a tree in a storm,
like the ground is moving away from the sea,
like the platelets are returning to kiss
each other again.
shake me like I need to be shook.

SWEET LITTLE DEATH

your words, gold-tipped
smooth maple syrup
dripping down my throat,
I savor these love-sounds,
the press
of your palms
against my smooth skin.
give me your golden, amber,
sweet-scented kisses, the scent
of caramelized sap burning
on your lips,
the cling of steam,
sugar evaporated
all over you,
and then me.
I would live inside you if I could,
crawl up your skin,
slide into your veins,
make a bed out of your heart,
you would be the sweet little death
I'd sink myself into.

STARLINGS

my love, he calls them
bad birds,

tells me farmers shoot them,
nuisance creatures that they are,
I don't say I understand,
because haven't you seen them
swell and swoop
cutting across the sky
like a maestro's arm?
bad birds.

everyone adores a robin,
a hummingbird, a blue jay,
but I can find a song in these little beasts,
could make a wish upon them.
bad birds

with such a sweet,
sweet name.

GAIA

I was gifted the world
and in return I gave it back,
split myself open,
swallowed what couldn't be,
cradled, cushioned, cared for all.
I am the myth, both brutal and
billowing with kindness,
giving you a hundred natural cruelties,
and gifting you a million times
that in beauty, a thankless job for all that.

what have you given me?
what have you taken?

each time I weep, who is there to
lay their hands, their bare feet,
against my hide, and say,
I am sorry, and *I love you?*
yet still I would lay myself
out for you, spread open, splayed out
unarmed, rest myself at your shoes, and tell you
the same things:

I am sorry, and *I love you.*

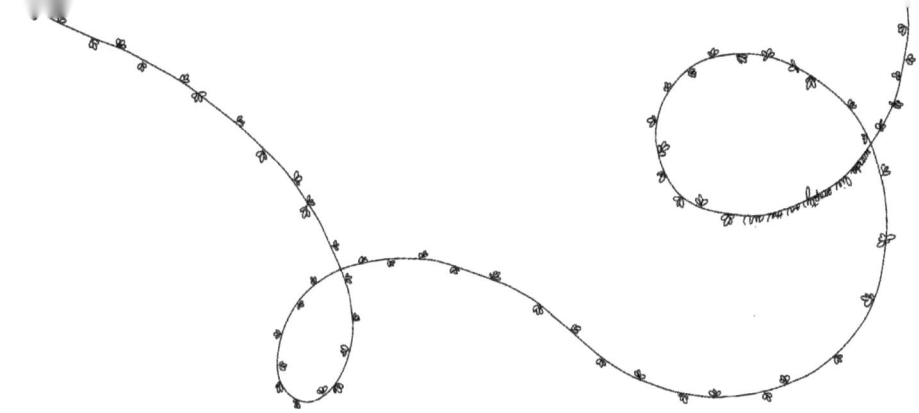

APHRODITE'S LAMENT

black-out poem, adapted from Collision by Duncan Thomas

I am haunted, or rather,
I haunt,
pleasure in detail,
a little carelessly,
my breath wrong.
pressing my cheek and breasts,
caressing agony,
touched and thrashing,
attraction.
stay, I prayed,
trembled an instant, but bent on,
pulled into this contact destruction.
the men set me low and sly,
leaving,
but now the sharpness of voices,
choked by low, familiar words, broken.
light and shadow
spread corners near the ceiling,
in the hollows,
words lie empty on the air.

CRAVINGS

don't give me
that soft talk,
those tender words,
I've spit out better dishes than you.
don't try to make me
choke down the
pretty gift you've shined up,
gleaming, round softness
like peaches,
don't make yourself sorry
that you tried.

I am not craving any love
but my own.

FLYING (MAGNIFIED)

I come from a time
when nothing flew
except birds.

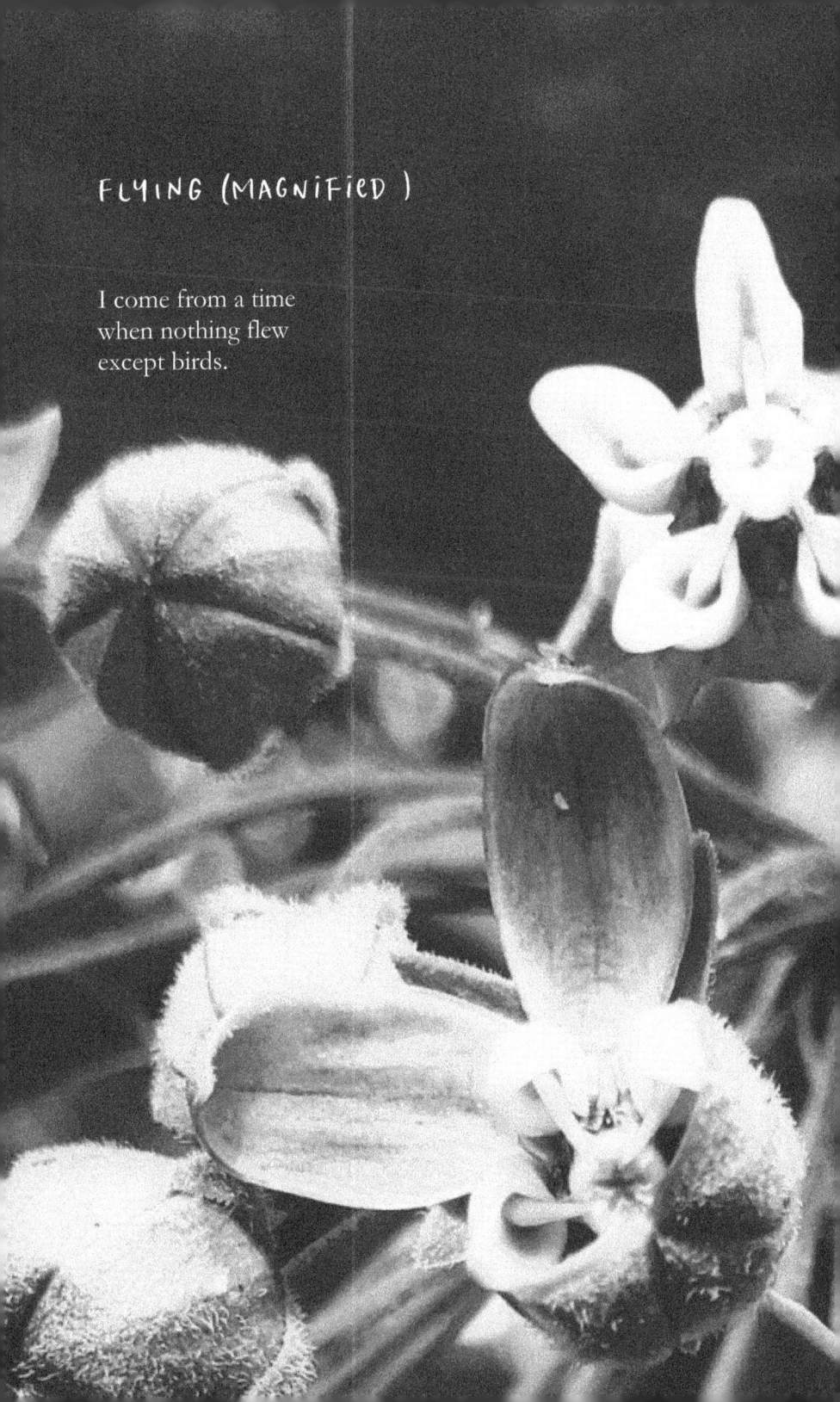

SHE KEPT SINGING

I now wear pink, my life's a joy,
I'm no man's queen, and no man's toy,
I sing off-key, I twirl my hair,
like it or leave me, I don't really care,
I walk around naked, I flirt and I tease,
I've no curse to answer to, I do as I please,
I own the stars, I dance and I pose,
silver rings adorn my toes,
I like to swear, I read and I write,
I painted my castle walls
tangerine-bright,
and no matter the tears that
I used to cry,
the wild within me
didn't wither and die.

STAR-CROSSED

come gently love, descend
yourself
upon me,
a blanket of flesh,
teach me the art
of love.
come swiftly, love,
lay yourself upon me,
heat me with skin
and lips,
show me the pleasure
of love.

DIANA
black-out poem, adapted from Your Long Hair *by Robert Tait*

your hair, the light

across

the ceiling,

what we have, touches,

bodies making light

of all we have done.

how slow sounds

can go

in the light's

undertow,

straining at a horizon,

a whole sense of us both

now, your long hair, light,

of light

away.

A SMALL COMPLETENESS
*black-out poem, adapted from This Business of Living
by Maurice Lindsay*

the river,
a wind,
roots of grasses
weave their symmetry and suddenly
twist out of element, a kick of air
recoiling under ripples, leaving,
torn to repair
and I experience
a small completeness.

SuCCuBuS

you left my hands

uncluttered,

and my mouth

hollow,

my thighs cold and trembling

with longing

for you to fill me

with all the things you'd taken,

and all the things

you never gave me.

MOODS

today the wind swept up our city,
touching down on country and town alike
to quietly remind us all that Mother Nature
can redecorate as she so chooses,
lifting garbage cans, and swirling leaves
until they sat, mounded in the middle of roads,
and stealing trampolines to bring them
from one yard to another.
as I sat in my car, a man crossed the street
with his two dogs, and his hat was taken
from his head as if with an invisible hand,
grabbing it just out of reach, so that he, panicked,
ran after it, dogs in tow, and finally snatched
it back from the playful wind to place back upon himself.
if I were him, I would have tucked it
under one arm until the wind was done
playing this game.
as it was, I folded myself against the chill
of wind to go into work, and when I came back out,
the wind was still, snowflakes gently curling
down in fat flakes,
as if *she* was saying, *there, there now.*

BEASTY

I am the winged crow,
I am the thorns on a deceitful rose,
I am too loud, too sharp,
too wild for polite company,
not a teacup, a doily, a bud vase,

I am the whole twisted briar plant.
I am not the beast you break,
I have already been broken
and been repaired.

see all my rips and tears?
only something strong can
survive such a wreckage,
only something strong can
see how destruction tastes,
can spit it back out again with a smile.

I am the wild, the broken,
the beautiful mess of ruin built back up again,
and again, and again.

BONES

un-bone my form,
skeleton soft,
languid in your arms,
I am not yours for the taking
I am only mine to give.

tonight there is power in giving,
tonight you can take my frame away,
build a graveyard
out of all my hard edges,
I won't need it where we go.
leave nothing but my organs pulsing, wild fluid,
bleeding red with lust.

I would rather be a secret held against you
held up with nothing but your bones.

SIDESHOW

you were laid across his skin,
shaped yourself into a tiger,
an anchor, a heart stuck through
with three arrows.
you were a curtain shut tight
across his ribcage,
a sparrow on his neck, fine-feathered wing
just fluttering
near his perfect right earlobe.
you were moored
to his being, fixed at every spot, a blend
of night-black and cobalt,
a wink of crimson, dash of canary-yellow
against his tight honey-skin.
you were speckled like a constellation
across his lean forearm, a cat-grin
when he flexed for the other girls.
you were there, the soft wide
of his pupils echoed in the blue rose you curled
into on his hip.
you were so near it was hard to tell
where you ended and he began,
and now, I see, he is removing you...

"*actually*," she interrupts me, "*I am removing myself.*"

charmed

crystals * the smell of lavender * citrus * thinking good thoughts * spell books on the coffee table * crossing my fingers * touching glass over railroad tracks * 11:11 on my clock * blowing birthday candles out with my eyes shut * reading the secret * positive visualization * the almond cookies I make on full moon nights * handwritten spell-poems I've written since my adolescence * hope * bluebirds * wishing on a star * manifesting my destiny * praying for someone else * meaning it * wanting so much * being grateful for what I have * biting my lip with need * making my own path * asking for more * giving more all around * realizing love is magic * white light surrounding me * knowing myself * angels in the corner of one eye * my hushed breath * longing flowing in my veins * the hum of power * when I find my magic again * when my magic finds me *

I ASK FOR LOVE

I ask for love.
all around my house are
bowls of stones,
baby-pink quartz,
to bring love here,
to ask it to stay—to invite it
to live here, too.
I collect sweet thoughts and
hopes for an earth brimming
with white light and the easy
peace of calm.
I ask for love, I pray, I cry,
love
love
love, please live here.

3

unlock these prisons
from my wrists,
breathe new air into the space
between me and the curving
roof above.

speak to me, not of what I can do—
no, those words have been repeated for as long
as the sky is deep—
tell me instead all the ways
in which you'll give yourself and everything else
to me.

for once, let me be the top of the night,
let me loop
my fingers 'round your wrists.

let me be the wish you don't need to speak
let me be all three of them.

SNOW WHITE

snow white, lips red,
don't be the one
that waits in bed.

wake yourself.

THE MAGICIAN'S KISS

black-out poem, adapted from To G Occasionally
by Thomas A. Clark

kisses break

your lips,

as if rolling

through the pain.

DREAMS

I will dream big dreams,
I will be the bearer of grand news,
I will be the singer of songs,
the kind that breaks your hardened heart
into tears.
I will carve from the sky stars
that light up whole worlds.
I will be the wonder of your night,
the lover of your life,
I will be the enchantress you
sculpted in your sleep,
the bewitcher who casts your needs,
I will be the paintbrush, the wand,
the crystal ball you gaze into and
can't tear your eyes away from,
I will be what you
can't ignore,
the dreams that blind you
which you accept
gratefully.

because I am good for you,
I am the flow of awe back into your life.

WISHES COME TRUE

thrice, rounded, full,
I cupped
my hands, life flowing
within me,
and it was like holding a wish
under my skin
each and every time.

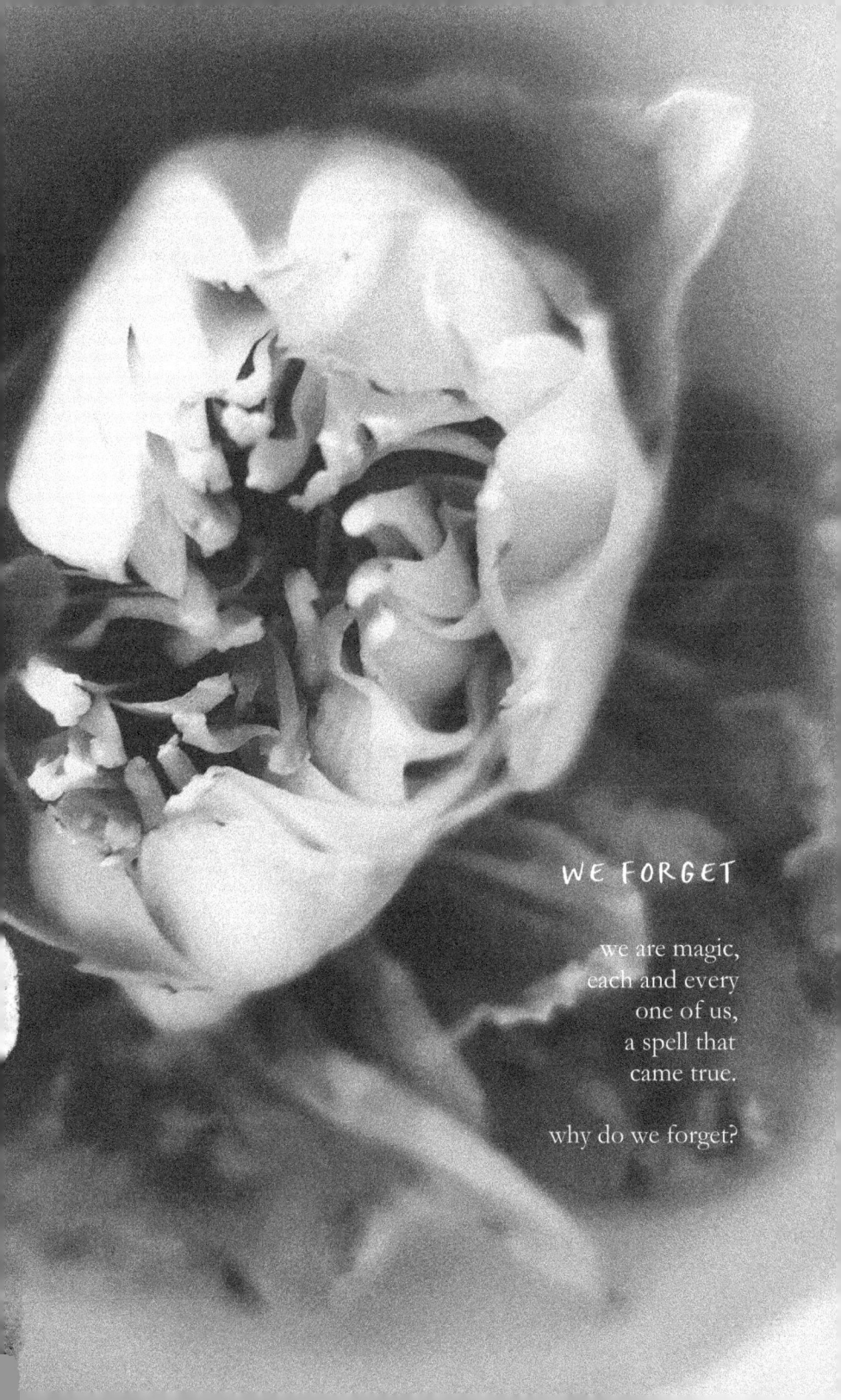

WE FORGET

we are magic,
each and every
one of us,
a spell that
came true.

why do we forget?

GROUNDING

me, who has need
of the earth now,
whose soul cannot contain much more (of the pain),
pleading, *help me, please help.*
pull from the bottom of my feet
a band of roots,
which anchor me down,
which grind me here.
give me something to clutch,
something to remind me that I am safe,
solid, I belong,
that I should not—cannot—just float away.
give me roots, hold me here,
hold me.
hold me.

TAKE ME

take me with gold,

take me with light,

take me in day,

take me at night,

brush yourself,

feather-touch kiss,

give me a tender love,

magic I'll miss.

MAGIC WORDS

I reread *A Thousand Mornings.* I reread *Lace, Bone, Beast,* I
reread about Alice and the Hinterland, about the light princess,
about Beauty—or rather, Honour. I reread the lyrics of the
songs I've heard a thousand times, I sing along, I cry along, I
pick out script for my next tattoo, I ink myself with poetry, I
make my skin a tribute, I read the old words, I read words
locked in a grid, I find my spirit within these places, I make a
church out of my bookshelves, I look to these writers as a
beacon, as a bouquet, as a memory board, as a collected hope.
their words render me breathless, the syllables stun me silent,
and for someone who has so very much to say, that is quite the
feat.

SATURDAY

Saturday, and I'd set aside the days for wellness,
a weekend of falling back in love with my words
marked it off on my calendar, seizing hours
for self-care, and is it any wonder, rebel that I am,
that instead I managed only half of what I'd gifted myself?

why, when I want so hard to find this good
do I insist on clinging to old curses instead?

LOVE SPELL

I am under a love spell
and I cast it myself,
I cast it *for* myself.
I am yours, absolutely,
without pause, without hesitation.
I'll be yours with magic,

I'll be yours long after
it fades away.

A THOUSAND WAYS

I could think of a thousand ways to say
that my heart beats in tune with yours.
do you know that's what I mean when I write poetry
and your face comes through in it?
do you know that what I mean when I say
to God, to the universe *thank you*,
and it's true each and every time?

TRUE LOVE'S KISS

feeling your kiss erases the time,
gives me a song, a wish, and a rhyme,
your lips upon mine make me feel complete,
your mouth upon mine was never so sweet.
kiss me and kiss me, my knees are so weak,
please just kiss me and don't even speak,
kiss me and kiss me 'til time passes by,
kiss me and kiss me, and don't ask me why,
kiss me until the time passes on,
kiss me until the ache is long gone,
kiss me and hold me, again you are mine,
kiss me and kiss me, you're sweeter than wine.

ever after

realizing I've grown up * realizing I'm still growing * trying to get through the hard days knowing what I now know * trying not to regret anything * adulthood * bills and homework * reading fairytales aloud * trying to remember how I felt then * pushing myself * wondering if I'm good enough * still struggling * knowing true love * giving it to myself, too * telling my body I'm sorry * being gentle * being firm * finally having a sense of self * understanding my own identity * wearing whatever I damn well please * cutting my hair how I like * cutting out unhealthy people * saying good-bye to ghosts * beauty after being broken * living life * seeing death * wanting to see it all * a full heart * peonies cut fresh from my garden * hummingbirds in jewel tones that watch me through the window * aqua cuts of glass * soft edges * crying on the couch * a broken wash machine * princess movies * singing old lullabies * take-out on a Tuesday night * being so tired I think I'll shut down * wanting to wake up * slow-dancing in my living room * making magic out of moments * cooking on the weekends * the sweet smell of a clean baby * white laundry on the line * embracing * a blue house * rolling green hills * my loves * my life * me * and you *

KING

princes don't faze me,
hello, good-bye,
a stately king has caught
my eye,
and I don't care
what princes do
they'll never be
as good as you.

SPINNING WHEEL

weave into your life
threads of unbreakable
good—
it is the only way
you will call yourself
happy.

WE WALKED IN SPRING

do you remember how we walked in spring? I think even now
I catch the milk-white blossoms from the corner of my eye, the
apple-tinted leaves that fluttered over us as we strolled.
beginnings are a kind of magic, the way time slows and then
rolls into something else. what a beautiful life we've already
had, blossoms strung overhead like garland, the green snap of
air like breath against our untouched cheeks, we were love
undone and gentle-wild, we were as perfect as the flowers and
the sky. do you remember how we walked in spring?

BATTLEFIELD

don't ask me to be the strong I was before.
I've softened for myself,
and I like it that way.
I will not battle against my truth
in order to please someone
who'd rather see me blood-strewn
than tender.
I can see the hard parts
of me
for what they were
then—armor,
and I choose to reveal myself now
naked, vulnerable, a breath amidst
the cries,
a lily among the battlefield.

MY HEART HAS A VOICE

this thing is not all neat / packaged up / soft-curved
and symmetrical /easy to draw / easy to train or to break /

it is not simple / not even pretty / not a target for some
dangerous archer /but the arrow itself / not an organ but a
soul / a mirror / a hand / a lesson failed and finally learned /

but forgive my contradictions / I'm trying to say yes / yes I do
find it beautiful after all / look how soft / it has been broken
and repaired too / it has been the weapon and the wound /
but it is still alive / a feral beating thing / a quivering lovely gift
/ mine to give to you / yours to give back again / mine to take
/ to fix / to root / to let it grow
where it will grow / to let it breathe and bleed and speak /

listen / can you hear it / my heart has a voice / and you make
it sing.

ETERNAL SUNSHINE

kiss me like
we're
becoming
strangers
once again

TRUE STORY

instead of a feather
today, I stepped over a wing—a *wing*
ripped from a bird
somehow, probably some horrid way,
but instead of stitching myself
to this gruesome tale
of some poor creature's fate
instead I'll muse
perhaps the bird removed it herself
maybe flight isn't all we make it out to be—
could being stuck on the ground
be somehow superior
to flying among the stars?
I've always idealized winged things,
angels, and fairies, and birds alike,
yet maybe that poor creature just wanted
to root herself to something,

maybe she wanted to be pinned
to something besides hope.
maybe somehow, the weight of it
was preventing her flight anyhow.

EMPATH

this world is the worst kind
of curse—not the softness in it, of which there is *some*,
but most of the rest—the jagged briars that will
draw from you not just blood but your very hope.
this world is the worst kind of curse,
the kind that will take every bit of ugliness
and exploit it, the kind
that will gut you with its wrongdoings.
this world is the worst kind of curse,
in it I have seen the face of death, and the smile
of evil, I have told myself again and again
that humans are not that bad,
that most of us are in fact good.
maybe that is a curse, too—

the fact that under all this agony
my heart is still
so soft.

THE WILD SWANS

on the edge of autumn,
they fly past,
that noteworthy event when someone
simply *must* say,
"the geese are flying south for the winter, huh?"
everyone's words
are on the season,

and here I am,
instead of pondering
grown-up thoughts of impending
mittens and slow-cooker stew, I'm dreaming
of a girl whose twelve brothers
turned into swans and flew
her across the sky
like a wish.

IMMORTALITY

we are nothing,
just specks of dust,
words on a page,
easily burned, easily erased.
we keep trying to ink
ourselves permanent,
to settle ourselves into the pages of
some book we don't even belong to,
but there is some kind
of wholeness to being finished,
to ending.
could we really do anything forever?

I couldn't,
except maybe love you.

ATLANTIS

yesterday, a tragedy.
yesterday, a clinic, because I couldn't breathe,
(this was before I even saw the news).
last week, my stomach curdling every bit of food,
not making me ill, just making me
not hungry.
yesterday, last night, my face wet,
fingers stabbing
letters into my phone,
Google-searching
all the ways I can remain in control,
a mother's instinct to keep
her children safe crosses species,
would make me cross oceans even.
yesterday, a tragedy,
and before that countless others,
too many others, so that they
blur into one another, so that
newscasters take minutes to name them,
so that I've already lost four pounds this week,
so that I wonder how our country will
pour the grief out and not sink
under the weight of it and start our cities anew
under water.
yesterday, today, tomorrow—does it matter when?
what is time when we are all
just one breath away from drowning?

RABBIT

some poets speak with their mouths, brave, words
flung like daggers, things to say.
I think I talk quietly. Lips shut. I talk with my hands, palms
open to show you how vulnerable, pressed
together praying, then fists clenched,
hidden in my lap, or fluttering, wing-soft.
lately it seems everything about me is soft, these hands,
this mouth, this belly, this heart.
some days, I wish I wasn't so frightened, a rabbit
amidst the thorns, unarmored.
some days I think even my bones are bendable,
think I'm not a flame, but the wax itself, melting, softened,
spread thin.

tell me all the things you love that are soft,
and I will answer there's a heap of ways it is not a good thing.
but like me, this poem is weak, and I have run out
of metaphors to mix.

in the end, what I'm saying is that I wish I had knives to throw.

SOME DAYS (MAGNIFIED)

my arms a castle,
I am the queen, the scullery maid,

I am the touch that everyone
bases their needs upon,

I am the cure, my hands the spell.
some days are everyone

taking from me
so that by the time I collapse
in the evening,

I am empty
of even myself.

TROUBADOR

here is your money back / here is the royal acclaim
I've earned / from all these years of singing so small /
I cannot give music to your courts / I cannot make
these notes sound less hollow / like an accordion / I am
pleated with misgivings / heavy with the layers of longing
/ how can I sing / of one pretty boy / or one pretty girl /
or any pretty soul indeed / knowing I am sick with need /
for the whole wide world / to press itself with
some softness / against my broken skin?

QUICKSAND

I was there when they were new,
five-sided, sharp points
tipped towards the sun.
I was here again, obsessed
with gold-winged liner,
black as night sheets laid across
my shoulders,
white orchids that weren't really
orchids at all,
the lapis of a hot desert sky.
I was there then here and many
lifelines in between.
I do not know the myths,
I only know my heart, throbbing
to reach across
centuries,
risking my lungs to drown
in the quicksand
that comes with memories
I don't even own.

TENNESSEE

last night, you curled into me,
sleepy smile, reaching,
I counted my blessings by your breaths,
your heart
under my hand.
this morning, your soft
stomach turned itself inside out,
and I ran a bath afterwards to rinse
off the sick.
you swam in turquoise water,
belly down, long hair unfurled
behind you, like a mermaid
in the sea.
right now, we sit together, quiet,
your fingers wrapped around mine,
sunflowers at my feet,
sun streaming butter-yellow through
this borrowed room, and I
count my blessings once again.

NIGHT'S DREAM

under the sky we laid out a blanket,
and on our backs, we, side-by-side,
watched the night
as stars emerged from
the blanket of black.
each sparkle above had us pointing *look, look at that one.*
with patience we studied
the openness above, waited
for the stars to fall from the sky.
I was your Titania, queen underneath
the spangled ceiling,
and you brushed your hand against mine,
reminding me
how large a small thing can be,
and I did not make a wish that night
I did not even need to.

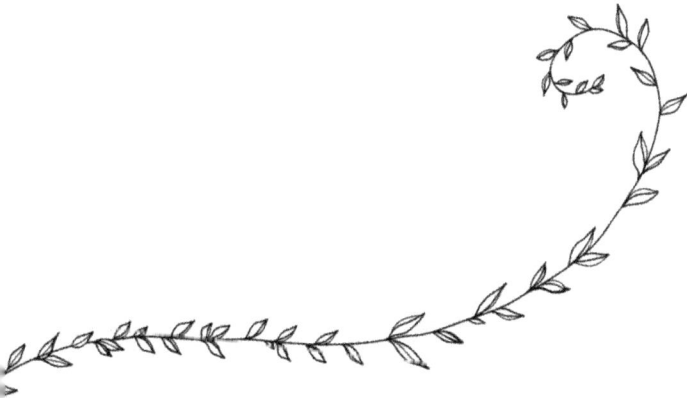

CINDERELLA

I am not so much a queen
as I'd like to think, and only *once*
someone on Instagram called me that—*Queen*
—because she liked my words,
but in real life (the moments between icons),
I am more like Cinderella before the slippers:
dusted, sooted with well-meaning,
dirty hands from so much
cleaning, cleaning up,
not just after myself,
but after everyone else,
and occasionally, eyeing the
jagged mountains of laundry
do I think,
Cinderella has got nothin' on me,

THE MUSE

on a Sunday, in May
she dropped on my lap one perfect, green leaf
edged like lace, wide enough to shade my face
from the sun,
smooth enough to rub against my tired cheek
pretty enough to paint.

in the chill of a two-a.m. morning,
on my way to the kitchen for a glass of water,
she cast the moon just so into my open windows,
and all the way back to my room, throat wet with relief,
I thought I'd never seen anything
so pure as that disc staring at me through the glass,
and how someone should write about it.

my youngest child tugged on one finger, mouth sticky
with jam, pigtails askew, said something clever
and sweet, something that made me think I should
get out my old camera, capture that moment before
the jam got washed away.

but I didn't.
but I didn't.
but I didn't.

AN EVER AFTER

let loose upon me the bare grasps of
morning,
the eagerness of breath on a cold night
unfold me with your need,
swallow whole fears of mine
so I never have to feel them again,
curl yourself around my life
so that I hardly know
where I end and you begin.
give me the
ragged beauty of an
ever after that is
magic in and of itself.

MAGIC

they used to slip from me,
those words,
yet they never felt like me,
the way you wear ill-fitting clothes,
the way you hide under hair that
isn't quite right,
the way at sixteen, nineteen,
even twenty-five,
I had yet to learn myself.

as decades roll away
into present and I am left
with this empty feeling of
still searching for what fits,
I realize I find myself suited in a different belief,
one I'd forgotten long ago—the one I'd told
myself I couldn't have.
I find myself now
in the moon, in the space
between childhood dreams and
the way I felt wild in my skin
and now, in the all-too-adultness
of everyday living, but as someone who still
finds allure in the sky

I will take whatever magic I can get,
I will make it myself if I must.

PHENOMENAL
(after Maya Angelou)

it takes me thirty-some years to say this,
not the thank you part, not to *her,*
but to me, the part that needs to know this,
that has to know it.

it takes me thirty-some years to notice
there are moons on my fingers, and stars on my face.
did you know (because for so long I didn't)
my little toes curl like seashells?
and you could say my ears are shaped the same—
what is that if not phenomenal?

for so long I focused on the way I lacked,
the way I failed to meet a set of expectations.
even now I could say *ugh*
because lines stripe my belly,
where I carried three full-term babies,
where I lost several others.
but isn't that a kind of magic right there?
a kind of badass, *fuck-yeah magic,* to say I didn't break
apart at the seams?
I am still here, even if I sag sometimes.

do you see me? do you see yourself? you're here, too.

thirty-something, and finally there's good that
isn't impossible to see,
like these hips, my hips, wide enough to perch
a child, wide enough to hold the world.
my breasts, for feeding, for pleasure, to catch my lover's
eyes even after all this time.

this body, these arms inked,
no longer smooth, my legs, pale but muscled-soft.
I can walk on these legs.
I can *dance* with them.
I carry myself anywhere I want to go, and some
places I don't.

my body, my body, what a body I have been given.
what a beautiful body I will give myself.
instead of closing my eyes to my flaws,
to the things imperfect, the list that never shrinks
(just like my waistline, *ha*)
I will open them wide, say *here*, open myself up all vulnerable
to you,
to me, in front of my children especially,
know that I am good enough.
I am more than that, even.
this body, a work of art, a broken mess—
and who's to say one is better than the other?
I will take all of me at once.
I will give this gift again and again.
there is beauty in all the things that made me disappear before,
that made me erase the lines of who I was, and who I dared to
be
there is beauty in accepting this.
there is beauty all over me and all over you,
whatever you are made of,
whatever you've built out of yourself.

say it with me, now,
say it out loud: *phenomenal.*

EVERY BOOK IS A SPELL BOOK

this tiny book is like a jewel,
better than a ruby or sapphire.
it is words, magic ones.
my own pen drips
with them. and someday,
someday I'd like to have a
mini-jewel book of my own
browned pages,
silver embossed,
tattered corners,
floral embellishments,
someone else's name scrawled
inside, a possessive
owner too frightened to lose
my words,
more precious than treasure.

ENCHANTED

I have spent nights on the bathroom floor, days hiding my bare body under the comforter of lovers I didn't love. you know how people add up mundane task, and tell you thinks like, you'll spend four years of your life folding laundry—do they ever say how much time you'll spend crying? sometimes it feels I've wasted decades weeping. does it matter how much I have lost myself and hated myself and learned myself and lost yet again? does it matter that I have screamed to God and I have cursed my heart beating? I live on, don't I? so, does it matter? that I've bled my own babies out? does it matter how many times I fucked myself over? under? thoroughly and completely?

I'm still here, aren't I?

Let me lay myself out a different way, say instead, that I have laughed so fully it was as if the goddess of joy herself had whispered in my ear, that I've cried tears of utter and complete thankfulness, and meant every single drop, that I have held life in my hands, that I have held death, too, and you know what? I'm not even sorry. I have found healing and a place of peace, and I like it here. I finally understand, and I hope one day you do, too. I hope someday you will see your life spread out behind you, and be able to call it—as a whole—enchanted. I hope you will believe yourself when you say it.

ROYAL SEAMSTRESS PART 2

I have unraveled myself
too many times
to get all tangled up no

THE FOUNTAIN OF YOUTH

my one living grandmother
is ninety-eight years old,
and compared to her I
am young
though somedays I feel eons have
come and gone around me.
still, I remind myself I have a whole
lifetime yet to live, probably,
and drunk-text-messages from
high-school friends tell me, "don't grow up yet."
which is both sweet and sad
because isn't it too late for that?
how can you regain nativity when you've
seen and felt such adultness pressing all against you
in colors of beige and bland?
but they are on to something, my heart
says, so that I recognize the ringing
of this want, for me to reach beyond
bills, and dishes, and health insurance,
so that I can answer, "don't worry, I won't."
and mean it.

this lives in my pores, glaring in the light of
my hazel eyes, set wide, not so much from green
but from hope, the way I still try to catch
the glimpses of fairies in our woods, or strain
my ears against a cockle shell in a stranger's bathroom
it is there, the need of what I used to see all at once,
the twinge of it, in the swell of my skin against my
clothing, on my words, in my thoughts,
something I teach my children already.

don't grow up yet.
how could I?

there's so very much left to stay young for.

DEATH

black-out poem, adapted from The Shell by George MacBeth

since the shell took you in its arms,
body of light,
flowers of the sea (not one I could call ours),
that ocean you were remains,
through darkness, your swell,
your skin.
I dream I hear dead tears,
strained weeping that stuns.

stars clear out of this evening,
to what has gone beyond
through cold, your breaking
body, that flood of
mourning…

I turn to go, shadows merge
and blur
the flow of death.

REINCARNATION

we drift in and out of
our own words,
we draw breaths up and out
of chests that are
heavied, hollowed cages
what is it tugging us back
again & again?
what is left to conquer of this earth
lifetime after lifetime?
my romantic heart says, "*love; we have
yet to learn it.*"
and I'm afraid to tell myself
this addition, "we cannot conquer love, we can only
surrender to it."
how many more lifetimes will it take before we learn
that this is true?
how many wasted centuries have we spent
trying to make big words
out of something so simple?

APOLOGIZING

have you ever heard some people speak? how
I'm sorry
if it's not too much trouble
I don't mean to bother you
fills up their speech?
lately I catch myself
I'm sorry
catch myself folding up to be smaller
catch myself hating on this voice
this body, and I'm tired
of apologizing for the space I take up
tired of apologizing for this hunger
these dreams, this ambition, this lipstick still drawn crooked,
these clothes, the loud music I still shake my ass to,
and youth is overrated anyhow.
look how young I feel, how much joy
I've found again!
I'm practically a child running
after the ice cream truck, practically giddy with the knowing
of myself, with the accepting of who I am, and
who I'm still becoming.

it took too long and yet was nothing at all,
my years an eyelash, a poem, a blink,
my next birthday I'll be 37 and oh how quickly time goes by,
a flash, a dozen heartbreaks and five thousand
memories I'd erase if I could and fifty thousand more, I'd love
to relive, or maybe that ratio is all wrong, and maybe
I'm still all wrong but at least
I'm finally learning
how to stop apologizing.

SUGAR PLUMS

bells twinkling,
lights winking,
snow-dusted treetops,
branches thick with white,
Jack Frost's work, like an open hand,
across the windowpanes.
from the kitchen, scents—cinnamon, orange zest,
vanilla beans, black seeds smudged
on my fingertips,
homemade maple syrup, cocoa powder
hanging on the air, settling
on my skin so that I smell like
a truffle, a macaron, chocolate ganache.
and there are sounds, too—the crinkle
of wrapping paper, the crunch of
snow beneath our boots, the Nutcracker
soundtrack, a pas de deux
soft and kind in my ears.
and in my eyes, the sight of them,
smiles lit on their faces,
wonder made manifest,
one tiny thing bringing to mind
a hundred other joys.

MERMAID SOUL

me / half-mermaid / who really doesn't swim all that well / or all that much / but revels in the warm embrace of water / who is soothed by waves / by the sweet smell of rain / the brine of oceans / the sharp seaweed-rich odor of lakes / who soaks in bathtubs until my skin protests in puckers / who sprays salt in my hair / who will tattoo rivers on my wrists / tell me I am not some kind of water witch.

WHAT WILL I TELL MY CHILDREN

what will I tell my children
when they ask me
if dreams come true?

like, sorry, there is no singing with
birds perched on your
outstretched hand, nor are there
jewels and gowns and riding off
into the sunset like there always is
in movies where we lie to ourselves—
more likely to have the words in our
mouths turn to dust than
soprano beauty in a forest,

and sorry, there are no
wings or swans or happily ever afters,
or not the way we've been told
not the way we've been expecting
but.

but I will tell them
if you are lucky
you will have something like how I feel
when I look at you, and yeah
there are miracles and that is
good enough for me.

LiKe WATER FoR CHoCoLATe

an ode to Tita

apron tied around my waist,
I almost catch the scent of her—

spiced tea, rose petals,
fried dough, sausage and
sardines,
sugar and salt,

can almost cook like her, too
so that when I make something with love
it is palpable on the tongue,

almost like I'm there with her, too
in a book, on the page, on a ranch
down in Mexico,

almost like her strong hands are
guiding me as I sustain life,
as I find a way to make it beautiful.

DECORATING CASTLES

today, let us say we are
glorious,
let us not wallpaper the dots
from our skin,
not paper away the scars that run like
warnings, telling stories all along us.
today, let us not try to downsize,
to expand,
today, let us be castles,
rich with tradition, with history,
full of secrets, some tightly guarded,
some exposed for all to see,
today, let us be decorated with love—not *disappointment*—so
that if one of us wants to paint our walls with tubes
of red, and one would rather fling
open the curtains, reveal naked truth below,
that both choices are fine—both come from a place
of joy.
today, let us play within these walls,
let us proclaim, perhaps we know
almost nothing, but at least we know ourselves.
today let us love those shelves, those walls,
our selves,
today, let us be glory itself.

HINDSIGHT

looking back at myself
how could I not wish
I would have loved myself
more?

how could I not see myself
in your eyes now,
and not be wounded on my
own behalf?

every time I love you, I love
myself more, all the scraps and
scrapes of me, all the bones laid bare,
how could I not say
with all honesty, how fucking brave
I had to be, how strong,
how beautiful, how perfectly, imperfectly
magical, how red my blood, how soft
my heart,

look at it now, spilling over with thanks,
with admiration, not just for you, not just
for what I've become, but for what it took
of me,
to get here.

I FIND STILLNESS

I find stillness / bare skin on the earth /
as you laugh
in the background / sun breaking
through the leaves

and I think / there could never be a way /
to match this perfect moment /

never another thing /
that tastes as sweet as this sort of peace.

A MORNING

we find shapes in the clouds, flowers, on the shadowed

pavement. stars in each other's eyes. darling, my darlings, look

what you've made out of my life. look

what you've made out of me

WILD MAGIC

if you let it, slowly, it will go
with enough time, enough distance,
the way a relationship dies with lack
of attention,
the way a plant withers
from lack of care.
if you let it, it will seep out
of your pores,
will uncoil itself from
your essence and wrap onto
someone else.

but if you feed it, surely, it will grow
it will dig its roots deeper
so that enchantment spreads
from your very smile.
if you feed it, nurture it, revel in its whimsy,
it will cling to your skin,
your eyes will light up
the way you never knew
a non-child's could.

if you feed it, this wild magic,
it *will* eventually break you apart with all the
expectations, and all the truths that come with age.
it is not the same as it was then

it is stronger, it is surer
it is the way you step after falling
knowing that you can get back up again.

it will prick you like a thorn,
but you will love it all the more.

the ups and downs of it will
grow with you like a vine that stops
and surely starts back up again.

if we let it bloom,
our wild magic will
be a garden that never
ceases to grow us into something
that is good, and fierce, and
heaving with hope.

water it, feed it, let it blossom.

we are not too jaded,
are we?

for a bit of magic?
for a whole lifetime of it?

the end

ACKNOWLEDGMENT

There are so many people who helped me to create this book, and everyone was lovely.

First, let me thank Jamie McLachlan, whom I can always count on for honest critiques, writing advice, and who beta-read this manuscript in its messiest stages. Thank you to my other book besties, Kelly Cain (who also helped reformat for the second edition!), Bianca M. Schwarz and C.H. Armstrong, who are all incredibly supportive.

Thank you to the wonderful authors who blurbed my book in its initial form: Shelby Leigh (who also beta-read), Morgan Nikola-Wren, Molly Ringle, Marya Layth, N.L. Shompole, and my dear friend Autumn Lindsey.
Thank you to Ampersand book's stunning cover design, and everyone who had a hand in the technical formation, from the original formatting by Whitney at SGR Publishing to Cheyenne Raine at Raine Publishing for the second edition.

Thank you to every reader who has bought, shared, read, supported, and/or encouraged any of my work. Thanks for every kind review, every shout-out, every Bookstagram picture. I truly appreciate you all. And to every writer and artist who inspired this book.

Thank you to wonderful friends, family, and everyone who has championed my work from day one. Thank you especially to my parents, whose support is truly unmatched.

And lastly, to my own little family, who provide me with endless inspiration, but most importantly- love. You are all my happily-ever-after.

ABOUT THE AUTHOR

Amanda Linsmeier has been a book nerd as long as she can remember, and it was that great love of reading—especially R.L. Stine books and fairytales—that brought her to writing her own things. A self-proclaimed wimp, she finds courage in making up stories that scare her a little, and she hopes to scare you a little bit, too. She feels most joyful when writing, scream-singing her favorite songs, playing in the water, and laughing with her beloved family. She lives in a small blue house surrounded by trees and cornfields, with a man who smells like maple syrup and woodsmoke. Together they have three wonderfully wild children, and, somehow, five pets, including two dogs and three half-feral cats. At the time of this writing, a fourth cat is attempting to adopt her. His name is Mercury.

Her debut Young Adult novel STARLINGS will be published in summer of 2023. In the meantime, stay connected with her on Instagram @amandalinsmeier or check out her website amandalinsmier.com, where she will, someday, eventually, have a newsletter to send out.

WANT MORE?

Anthologies:
Deja You: Stories of Second Chances
Chasing Magic: A CWPH Anthology
Fireflies & Fairytales: A Fantasy Anthology
*[Dis]Connected: Poems & Stories of Connection and
Otherwise Vol. 2*

www.ingramcontent.com/pod-product-compliance
Lightning Source LLC
Chambersburg PA
CBHW031451070426
42452CB00038B/672